WAITING FOR

THE KING OF SPAIN

Diane Wakoski

Santa Barbara

BLACK SPARROW PRESS

1976

LIBRARY OF CONGRESS CATALOGING IN PUBLICATION DATA

Wakoski, Diane.
  Waiting for the King of Spain.

  I. Title.
PS3573.A42W3   813'.5'4   76-44512
ISBN 0-87685-293-2 (paper edition)
ISBN 0-87685-294-0 (cloth trade edition)
ISBN 0-87685-295-9 (signed cloth edition)

To all the Michaels

TABLE OF CONTENTS

I said to my soul, be still, and wait without hope
For hope would be hope of the wrong thing; wait without love
For love would be love of the wrong thing; there is yet faith
But the faith and the love and the hope are all in the waiting.

T. S. Eliot, "East Coker," Four Quartets

I. Waiting for the King of Spain

Beyond the Trunks of the Palm Trees

You fight some battle that scars your palms with old destiny;
a map of the moon
I once saw there. And now the lines have formed
marching armies
that crowd into our lives
like an invasion of the South Pacific.

                                        Yet, I have not
understood the change at all.
My eyes are still focused on the map of Mares & Plains,
like some water witch with my own hands
as divining rods.
I try to move towards
the spot I once saw marked "Plain of Diane." "Mare of Shooting Stars."
But that space is empty now.
Even the rows of khaki bodies I saw sweating in formation there
three weeks ago
have vanished.
No hand.
Only a print.

They teach that history is slow. The tyrannosaurus fossils
are millions of years old.
In spite of that, you seem to have vanished as totally
in three weeks,
and I am left
with my own hands quivering as they approach my face;

divining water there.
Or bending to some idea of it.

Beyond the trunks of the skinny palms, at my house,
there is the Pacific Ocean.
What does it mean
that someone
existed
once? Is not there now?

The lines in my own hands
have never changed.

Precisely, Not Violets

for the King of Spain

I only mark
the lonely ones, days when time slows down
and reminds me
of an ageing face.
I remember a girl with a bunch of wet violets
from a past
I do not know I lived.
And in this rain,
there is one footprint that does not blur;
the King of Spain,
following me,
invisible, of course,
yet not making me cry,
as you have,
M, the man who has left,
taking only the spider plant
and a french coffee pot, an antique table,
a marble ball,
an old inkstand,
and your clothes which used to fill many hangers.

Books, yes,
you took many books, but my house is full
of books. Books are my life. Grow in the corners
of my rugs and walls,
like violets in the spring.

I, too, am a book,
and you took the expensive hand-bound copy of that with you

to bury perhaps, under a stack of
fashionable volumes of new poetry.
But my house is still full of books,
in manuscript and folio,
bound and unbound,
and I, the original book always there
with too many publishers.

The word.
I live by the word.
You gave your word,
and now
have taken it back. Is that like a book going out of print?
Because no one will buy it?
If I could curse myself to silence
I would.
But without my tongue
violets would grow on the floor of my mouth and only
make you leave me
for different reasons.

And what have I lost
in losing you?
Not the King of Spain,
for he follows me everywhere.
A book, perhaps.
An idea.
The illusion that I could ever be loved,
as I have loved.
Or that love is any more
than a rabbit the hunting cats have mangled and left
on your back porch?

I only mark
the lonely ones, days writing out of a silence
someone not named Beethoven
put in my head.
Violets grow around my lips. Wet with
spring rain.

Their blue reminds me
of the beauty
solitary things
can have.

April Snow

The eye of the photographer
is mine.

When I look out of the window
I see the photo
of myself you took in a New York snow storm
10 years ago.
In it, I wear a long black shiny coat,
a Greta Garbo hat,
boots to protect my feet.
                              Today's snow storm,
I sit in a purple morning gown,
my white arms against the solid wooden table.
The house is blazing with yellow flowers,
while outside the only yellow object is the headlights of cars
moving slowly
through blowing snow.

The skeleton trees remind me
that winter's still here. One snow-laden pine
says winter's deep.
But it is April,
and two months since you left me. Though it could be
ten years. For "you" is only a character
in my dreams.

And Love makes me dream of you
every night,
but my dreams are nightmares. So, I have

filled my house
with books, steaming food, flowers.
A good wine
is drunk every night.
Music and poetry fill the air.
I live the good life,
surrounded by poets and musicians and painters.
Why I long for you or
wake up with those terrible dreams
I can't say.

Except that,
by the calendar it is spring.
April.
Yet, today it is snowing,
white, thick,

deep.

April snow.

In cold and texture perhaps
no different from January's frozen white.
But it seems different,
simply knowing
the robins have been here all week.
                                        By May
the tulips will have bloomed,
and I will be thinking of the ocean.
The King of Spain sends his greetings
to me:
            the broken branch,
            the patch of melted snow,
            outside my door.

A Shipment of George Washington Apples
Arrives in a Snow Storm

for Steve Brown

Roses on the snow,
bleeding out of my fingers, cut on the broken claret bottle,
and a thin memory,
from only yesterday,
of all the spring's crocuses,

               pale blue,
               white,
               gentian,
               yellow,

their heads so much larger than their bodies,
for they have practically no stems,
keeping themselves close to the ground,
in case April snows come.

The roses must have been in my head,
though surely the blood was not.
The apples, their crisp white meat showing through the red cheek.

And what was on Thunder Mountain tonight?
The King of Spain, sitting around some campfire,
thinking of salmon, of trout,
while the fire burned high,
the beans bubbling in the tin,
snow around the edges of his April too.

I wonder how to put these things together in my life:
    roses,

their blood,
the flowers of early spring, and
in the April snow, the King of Spain, with his gold doublet,
and one gold tooth, sitting at campfire,
in the American woods.
Thunder Mountain.
I hear this name in the distance,
and while it does not provide a clue,
it adds another voice.

Where is George Washington in all of this?
Eating an apple somewhere?
Trying to keep the
doctor away?

Looking for the King of Spain

Voices of women
like labels on familiar bottles
are in the corridor.
I, alone, in yellow kimono,
thinking of my dream last night.
I am still the naked girl
sleeping on an old chest with a quilt embroidered
with roses and signs of the zodiac.
There still hangs over my head
a sword.
Under me, in the chest,
are the bones of the dead.
And waking means I have to face my life
without you,
whom I so imprecisely tried to call The Man with the Silver Belt
    Buckle,
even buying you that buckle
to keep the integrity of legend
in my hands.

But, of course, you were neither Silver Man, nor the King
of Spain.
Only a man named
M,
just like all the others.

The voices of women
could have warned me,
or even that mysterious voice of your father,

had I listened.
But those voices
simply sounded
like corridor murmurs,
and I sat in my yellow kimono then too,
writing,
listening to the sounds like silk.

And foolishly,
I did not hear what they said,
for I was listening to music or perhaps
another voice,
one I thought was yours.
The King of Spain who often spoke words of love.
That alone should have warned me,
the voice wasn't yours.

My lover wears a cap of darkness.
You, M,
stand plainly there for all to see.

The voices in the corridor are quiet just now.
But I hear footsteps.
Are they your visible ones, M,
or this time will they belong to my real lover,
the man I spoke to
for so many years in darkness?

There are Lions like Yellow Dogs

There are lions, like yellow dogs, under
my feet.
              And burgundy thistles. A bird
for the lion's mouth.
The carpet I wish to walk on.
Described as Gashgai or Khamseh.
Seen only, in a catalogue.

Outside, the mountains of Santa Barbara are
blunted.
With fog.
The sun is beginning to burn off
the California day.
And already I am thinking of twilight.

A Chinese Dragon Tree
conceals orioles.
Marigold borders remind me,
it is the sun I love.

Gold,
orange,
red,
the yellow of lions.

And I keep coming back to your face,
thinking with love,
of its fine red-gold mustache.
The hair on fire with singing lions.

24

You made love (cut) to me (cut) in a brass bed, (cut)
polished (cut) like the sun.
I wish we had walked over lions, dogs, or birds.
But thistles
their purple needles catching in my wintry hair, clung,
and I, like the foolish woman I am,
(cut) cried after you left.

Not having learned
about departures. Or how to live with dusk,
my favorite time of day,
knowing
if the sun sets,
we must, then, make it rise
tomorrow.
Not trusting this to happen to itself.

Waking to the gold,
        orange,
        red,
        yellow
of your body,
wanting to wake to the gold,
           orange,
           red,
           yellow,

           gold,
           orange,
           red,
           yellow,

           gold,
           orange,
           red,
           yellow,
radiance of your body,
always holding me as I look to flowers,
lions, and birds;
wondering if such a day will come again.

Wanting not to love you,
but to have you.
For love implies loss.
And I need to believe
that without any act of will
or engine of enormous force,
that without me
the sun
would rise
every day. From my bed.

Wanting you to be that sun,
red-gold,
warm
in my bed each morning.
Knowing also
that the sun rises from the beds of half the hemisphere
each day,
and that it thus
logically
could never be
mine.

Is that a reason to choose darkness?
The lion roars,
startles me with its yellow dog face.
The dilemma of trying to accept
what you have told me.
Each new sun rising each new day.
But only
when you are there,
the warmth of love.
> Gold,
> orange,
> red,
> the yellow of lions.

> Gold,
> orange,

red,
the yellow of lions.

Gold,
orange,
red,
the yellow of lions.

Gold,
orange,
red,
the yellow of lions.

And Bishop Berkeley confirming
my fear: the sun might not
rise tomorrow morning.
And then
will I have the power
to imagine
another radiance /

                    The King of Spain.

Who is he,

when you are gone?

The King of Spain Eschews the Freezer

No,
    you say,
          speak out
          or not at all.
And I have diamonds hanging from my lips
as a retarded child wd drool.
No beauty.
The hideous reality. No control. You could not even have
compassion for.
                But diamonds
come this way.
And poison scorpions.
Along with 6 foot snakes.

If I said,
my heart is broken,
you would only (kindly) reply,
                   "Take care of yourself."
As if
I would really smash you,
were you a scorpion,
as if I would shoot off your bloody head,
were you that 6 foot rattlesnake,
as if you could understand diamonds when they fall from my mouth,
like milk down a careless baby's chin.
                 As if

love were something
anyone could
ignore.

Walking on the Beach at Laguna in the
Morning with a Man who has a Gold Tooth

The sandpipers scurrying,
   little piston legs mimicking the tide,
      we descend from flowered cliffs, the gazebo which holds
         a telescope for spotting whales, past an empty terrace which
            I've always felt should be mine.
                       Were it,
(mine)
              I'd be
       stretching inside the glass wall,
       drinking a morning pot of darjeeling,
       watching the Pacific in its inevitable motions,
and you would be fishing somewhere in the mountains,
or sleeping surrounded by a herd of antelope in the desert,
and I, mythically, walking, as I do in my head each morning,
on this beach with someone who is not
the King of Spain,
someone I know, who loves me, but who also
cannot be with me.

I think with sadness of walking alone,
but feel unreal when I wake up in the arms of a prince.
One should only wake up
in the arms of someone she's been with
for 40 years,
or at least someone who will stay there 40,
barring death.
             Yet, death has never

us
parted.
Me,
or any of the men whose arms I've awakened in.

Oh, Love, Love,
you are as mythic
as My King of Spain.

The Laguna Contract
(15 July, Laguna Beach, California)
to M.

Remember those mornings
on an island covered with bougainvillea,
honeysuckle, the rock rising
from blue sea, like some struggling giant's fist.

We drank (hideous) Nescafé
and wrote in fancy white-paged books.
But my body was as heavy with love, already,
as the later-summered apricot tree.
Needing,
so much needing to take yr love,
and like a dog with a favored bone
bury it somewhere that only I knew
to find it. A treasure,
and I so fearful someone would snatch it
away from me.

Only two years later
and you are gone; or I cannot find you
in that place where I thot you were
hidden.
Underground where maggot-pearls
and the glistening penis-red lengths of earthworm
are lying like jewels against the roots of
jacaranda, eucalyptus. No bone,
not even of contention.
Simply vanished.

Perhaps I have lost the location.
Perhaps the blinding yellow of shooting stars and lion's names,
the sunflowers, yarrow & aster
would not allow even me
to keep my treasures well-enough hidden
and buried.

Clarity is my passion.
Where is the night / dark enough
for secrets?

                                        Can I
really presume
anywhere
a cap of darkness?
one that allows invisible accompaniment,
secret views of other buried bones
nestling into loamy camouflage,
rotting and disappearing
or otherwise, secretly being dug up by the
neighboring dog,
carried away in sharp
ivory teeth
              to another hole,
perhaps
beneath that same summer-heavy tree
of apricots?

* * *

Remember sitting in a baroque hotel in Paris
drinking morning café filtre, the croissants so fresh
in their flakey buttery spiraling extensions?
I, so heavy with love,
like a massive solid oak armoire
or sideboard.
              You, who grew up with plastics,
not understanding, perhaps not even dreaming
there could be such weight.

Hard wood,
heavy tree limbs.
Years of ringing
wood teeth.
An old tree
that someone cut down and then lovingly
tooled,
shaped.
Remember,
Michaelangelo felt he had to go to the quarries himself
in order to properly cut out
the chunks of
heavy heavy marble
he wanted,
for the laborers had
neither his (yes, amazingly)
                          neither his strength
nor his eye.
And I wanted to keep hidden
my own clear, radiant feelings of love,
as a dog hides a bone.

* * *

David, my brother, gone over a cliff
and into the sea,
don't forget me.
Every wave crests white and
furious.
I watch for that feeling
of peace,
knowing only that you cannot keep love or lovers
from going away.
That you can bury your own bone,
but when you return,
it might be gone.

* * *

Remember,
waking up to the sky of Santa Fe,
so blue it made even your eyes stand pale in your head?
And drinking motel coffee
before starting on another day's brilliant journey?
The yellow contours of road
dry and precise as my lips.
But then too, I was heavy with love,
and while I did not see a runner with man's body and the head of a
wolf, accompanying the car's fast journeying, I did
not see him running along beside us,
smiling, showing his white teeth,
as another traveller in those parts did;

I could feel my heavy body
like the iron and steel of the machine we were driving in,
deprived of its features,
and collapsed into a giant shape
like a clenched fist.
Wanting to hang on to you.
Wanting to hold you forever,
yet somehow
always finding
I could not keep previous things
not even burying them in the rich black soil
of my life.
They would neither grow.
Nor would they stay.

On the desert,
large startlingly heavy meteors
have been found.
Stone.
Marble.
I am thinking of the man who could make David
(a more ancient David
than my brother)
out of marble.

Not burying

but revealing.
Another urge towards clarity.
Surely
the only circumstance.

* * *

Remembering pain
on this foggy morning under the cypress with
mourning doves and mockers looing and rattling
in the open windows,
the "M" on my arm branding me against
simple gratifications.
This morning the King of Spain is probably walking
on the grey beach
while I hold the beautiful curly head of some
perfect David
in my loving hands.
My body does not feel so heavy as my (simple) heart
does today. The "M" carved on my arm
glitters like a lightning bolt.
My landlord does not allow dogs here,
for, in burying their bones, they dig up
his flowers.
The sun always comes late
past the fog
at this time of year.
I'll be drinking coffee soon
with a man who has lightning painted over
his eyes, and we will talk to each other
about the love-skeletons we had buried
and which were gone or lost or rotted
when we came back to find them.
I will touch his body,
and remember how to keep love—
accepting it from wherever it comes.

He unclenches my fist.
In it are crushed yellow flowers I've been holding

all this time.
I throw them in the fireplace.
Tonight, we will build a fire
out of eucalyptus, orangewood and those wilted, crushed flowers.
Its radiance,
even I,
will not be foolish enough to try to bury
or hold.

Counting Your Blessings on all Six Fingers of Your Hand: A Vigil

*—this book of hours for all men
and women who wait*

Once again
4 a.m.
and I am tired but sleepless.
Waiting for your footsteps
in this rainy morning;
yet you have told me
you will never return.

Down on the rocks of our beach
there must be Wandering Tattlers.
I, of course, am in a strange place
but know that at home
there must be Mourning Doves
in the Cypresses.

Why are you leaving me?
You said you never would,
you, who rescued me from the jangle of my lonely bracelets,
just two years ago.
My mouth, my jaws,
they feel like iron—heavy and straining
in my moon face.
You say I've driven you away
and yet
what did I do,
but love you?

Love is an hour of exercise at Vic Tanney's
for a flabby man;
a steel wire holding your jaw
together;
a priceless wine
gone bad;
a body aching with winter flu.
I would hold myself alone
and wait for you,
as futile as it seems.
For, I love you
and have learned to accept love
like the scars
on my body—
representing the flawed parts of me
but also
my identity.

You are the man I love.
I need you in my house,
as I need fire,
I need good water to drink,
I need a little air to breathe,
I need
(oh, so banal)
your eyes that saw the indigo bunting
when I was looking on the
wet ground for mushrooms.
Once you loved me
for the moon in my fingers
but now it seems to have slipped
like some beautiful globe
of Tiffany glass, from its collar
and smashed itself.
I pick up the pieces,
wrap them carefully,
hoping some day my fingers
will be skillful enough
to repair.

Could you love me
if you saw all the little new moons
like puffballs,
pearls of faint geography
slipping from the earth
to my skin,
growing over me, as if I were a
rotting stump?
If so, then look,
they are there,
growing in the cold misty vapor
of my life.
I offer all these new ones
to you.
Come back.
This is a cry of pain.
And my name is not wolf.

The King of Spain knocks on
my door;
but I do not let him in.
I am waiting,
I do wait,
for you.

Reminded of One of Those Girls
I Never Was

Each night
I work late
washing dishes
or cooking for the next day
tidying floors
or closets
waiting for your midnight knock.
I go to bed finally,
alone,
under my yellow blanket.

Like the sun,
it shatters my wrists
and brushes my ankles.

The King of Spain
comes climbing through
the nasturtiums
in my window box.
Or perhaps I simply know
he is near
the pungent smell of the orange & yellow squashy
flowers.

He is not you,
of course.
His gold tooth making him distinct
from any of my other
lovers.

Perhaps you will never
again
knock on my midnight door.
The beautiful blond boys
I moon and yearn for
knock once
then return to their
bronzy girls.

This afternoon,
in the bar,
I saw the slim hand of a pretty girl
slip around your calf
as you stood next to her table.
And I too
wanted to touch
your serious tall legs.
But the nasturtiums growing in between
the narrow joints of my knees flashed
their yellow orange bitter ripe odor
then,

I felt covered with flowers.
I laughed,
talked loudly,
looked for my invisible
jealous lover,
the King of Spain to come walking
in the door.
I frightened myself with my own
compulsive talk,
wanting,
wanting,
wanting,
you.
Seeing that other hand move
around your calf
in such a gesture of familiarity.

Each night,
I work late,
reading,
sometimes writing,
waiting for your midnight knock.
But when it does not come
I turn off the lights.
My nasturtiums shrug their
waving silver dollar shoulders
and the squashy yellow-orange
flowers send out
their salad fragrance
into my night.

I have,
thank god,
I have
my faithful lover,
his gold tooth flashing like flowers.
The King of Spain.
And he loves me,
as you do not.
As no man ever has.
He is always there,
waiting, faithful,
more beautiful than the most beautiful blond boys in their
    linen sails.
The King of Spain
whom I met once on a California beach
when one dark man
was pulling a nail from his foot
and another was racing on a track with starfish.

Each night
I work late
waiting for your midnight knock.
And though I know you will never come,
I do not turn off the lights or
open my door,

even to the King of Spain,
until I know
it is too late,
and you are home sleeping
with one of those young
beautiful,
bronzy
girls,
one of those girls
who reminds me
of what
I never was.

Burning My Bridges Behind Me

for Terry Stokes

The sun comes in my morning apartment
like a flamenco dancer,
his heels making sharp edges on the flaming tulips,
bullets of winter light explode on my yellow cushions,
and the asparagus fern drips with green moisture, its delicate tendrils
curling with each click of the sun's
castanets.

Alone
now,
with only the sun as my lover,
and he invisible, as if we lived somewhere
East of the . . . and West of the Moon.

The way I denote him
is by starting fires. I burn the toast
in my oven while daydreaming about a cardinal flying through
a winter tree. My paper towels of yellow or red
catch on fire while I stand blazing
in a yellow kimono
hardly aware of anything but love.

The King of Spain, as usual mysterious, but letting me know
his connection with fire, sometimes burns his print
into the glass of my huge windows
and at night I watch the tip of one cigarette glowing
beneath the balcony where I stand
in the dark.

Once I dreamed of yr slasher and his secret acts
but realized then that I saw him only as
another beautiful dancer,
leaping from a rooftop, finally, to kill himself.
And that I wanted a banker, a yacht broker, the owner of a steel mill
or a metallurgist in the Andes
for my partner.
Men who took the world
and set it on fire. Who could not laugh at the sun,
foppish flamenco dancer that he is,
for he too was building an industrial nation, with each click of his
narrow boots, tapping sun onto my skin, glinting gold
into my hair, and that my crime
was not one of passion, but calculation.
Setting each bridge on fire, after I crossed it. Making sure each
gentle poet, or foolish cowboy, effete reader of beautiful books,
or blind photographer would not be able to cross back into
my life. For,
all the time,
I knew I wanted a banker, a yacht broker, the owner of a steel mill,
or a metallurgist in the Andes
for my partner.
Someone who took fire in his hands.
Who from a burning bridge
and a mountain
could forge some new metal
giving passage across the gap
into my life.

The King of Spain, who loves me,
with chests full of stolen gold and a head full of poetry
from the past, shimmers when he walks,
as the gold from his clothing gives off the precious light of fire.
He would not let a weak man walk in the door or out
more than once.

Each morning I wake up, the sun blazing
on the golds, yellows of chrysanthemum, marigold, poppy.

They are in my fingers, and I realize
how I sleep:

in a ring of fire.

My tongue is the flamenco dancer.
Which dances on burning bridges.
Which glows awake each morning
as gold light floods the fiery room.

II. Reviewing

"the new
  is the old
  viewed
  and reviewed,
  viewed over & over"

George Washington Meets the King of Spain
(on the Magellanic Clouds)

for John Martin

John,
no one understands
that I always have my tongue in cheek,
checking out all possibilities of my own foolishness.
Silence is the medium
for beauty.
I think this, walking through Barbara's beautiful carpeted rooms,
arranged by her own fingers of Lalique glass
and ordered into the serenity I search for in poetry
or music.
Heavens! Where did you think the Magellanic Clouds were, if not
in your own living room.
And surely, you know that when I wander through yr house
pausing to understand the muted amber or puzzled blue surface of
some opaque piece of glass, that I am looking
not for the King of Spain
but a glass slipper
I might slip on my tan foot
and walk elegantly out of the state of California,
wearing.
But of course
what I find is the print of the King of Spain by your swimming pool.
No, don't worry.
He isn't after your princess-like teenage daughter, whose tall
strawberry blond head is a little gold coin,

and whose hands will make bread for poets beside her mother's.
He's there, in exile, to follow me
and give me the sun in the form of a flamenco dancer, black-hatted
and tapping against my castanet lips,
with words of Peter Quince, arguments to Ramon Fernandez.
Even the clouds become shellacked and hard,
wood clacking together, little round gold suns moving in my fingers.

You wonder, in your white adobe walls, gleaming against the terra
    cotta roof,
all of Spain's wealth of arch and patio
curving into your books,
how I, the often silent daughter of the silent father of our country
come to your house to meet these men,
fathers, lovers, protectors, soldiers, captains,
my glass tongue like a bud vase
holding Lorca's bloody roses and the gardenias
of my own white face.
But they are what poetry is.
The exotic oranges and palms, the flamenco-dancing sun
beside the bunting of a stiff portly pearshaped president
understanding that we must each survey our own wealth
to acquire it.

And no, John, no one understands
my castanet tongue, in its cheek of fire,
clicking, laughing, clicking, laughing,
while I watch
from my window.
Waiting to see George Washington ride up on a chestnut,
to the King of Spain where he walks
in the landscape of my imagination,
and my tongue as fragmented as the rings of Saturn,
the grey rocks clicking together, as it moves,
laughing, clicking, laughing, clicking
when you say
               "go on to something new."

Not understanding,
that the new

is the old
viewed
and reviewed,
viewed over and over:
George Washington rides up.
His chestnut casts a shadow. The King of Spain looks up.
He stands in gold light.
My tongue of glass melts and becomes a tongue of fire.
It is in my cheek and I am laughing,
clicking the castanets of my uncle, the flamenco dancer,
of my lover, the sun,
dancing brilliantly into my morning window
with the sun,
the fire to which I am married,
the ring of it I carry with my keys,
the ring of fire I sleep in
waiting with laughter
for the same old thing, the only thing which is new,
love,
poetry,
music,

God, they all sit in your house,
the Magellanic Clouds weaving into your rugs,
ruffling the feathers of your cockatoos,
rippling the fans of your anemones,
keeping in control the fire of my tongue in cheek
that, yes, no one, John,
as you say,
understands.

Gold

for the King of Spain

I met you at the wrong time.
Your face was a pocket watch,
heavy and gold,
and I, a woman in a thin dress,
one with no pockets.

I fell in love with the train station,
the big clock hanging over
the crowd,
as the sun hangs in a winter sky,
or one yellow apple clings to the branches
at the end of
autumn;
        the crowd of us,
strangers,
       look up at it,
like many spools of different-colored thread in a basket;
the big scissors, a train, pulls in,
and we are cut away from one place,
stitched along the track to another.
I watch that clock,
knowing I will not meet you here in this train station,
but I imagine you are
zipping the back of my dress up,
before I leave in the morning,
touching my bare arms,
and we drink our coffee, looking out the window

at dawn,
painfully telling time
by the sun
which has become a big pocketwatch,
too hot to hold.

I asked you for directions yesterday.
Your face was
a compass
with a pointer, branch-like, temperamental & skitterish,
moving around from E to N,
erratically,
and I was looking for the South,
because I need warmth and sun,
and I was afraid of your Northern aspect,
fall and wintery,
a bare tree,
a mountain with snow,
a cave of ice,
an avalanche,
but I saw
my own hands,
as gold indicators, slender,
moving imperceptibly,
around the same small set of also gold numbers each year.
And the ancient stem which moved them
even thinner,
hidden by my own face.

I met you at the wrong time.
Too late for love.
Your face was a gold pocketwatch, reminding me of the past,
a compass showing that I had no magnetic North,
only the true directions found from stars;
the lonely map and time that astronomers
record.

Some Constantly Besieged Castle

Note: the lines "Next time we meet, / let's keep our clothes on" are from a poem presented in one of my poetry workshops by a New York poetry student named Binnie Klein. I was so tantalized by the lines that I assigned everyone in the workshop to try to make a poem out of them. I felt they were a good example of useful lines buried in a bad poem. Alas, I was the only one to do anything further with them, but am grateful to the workshop for giving me the opportunity to make this poem.

Next time we meet,
let's keep our clothes on.
Let's not touch,
letting our bodies be like seashells
empty of soft mollusk life,
or even a hint that it's a possibility.
Let's not even spend the night
in the same city,
for surely I would come tiptoeing to your door
in the middle of it,
in spite of my good intentions,
like water seeping under the sill,
a quiet flood breaking over your large
sailor's body, as the
phosphorescent wake behind a slim boat.

Let's not be in a room alone:
we might fall silent as a deserted barrier reef
and turn into coral hunters.
Scratching hands and legs in an attempt to break off
pieces of our own simple body stone.

Let us surround ourselves with others,
so that we can talk passionately
about the subject of love,
showering sparkling drops around the room,
without soaking each other,
                              as groupers,
big sea bass, travel the seas,
with many smaller fish swimming along
for the nourishment.

Next time we meet,
let's both be married to other people
and not in danger of being on rafts alone
in the Atlantic.
Because your naked body
excites me as if
I saw a vision of a Spanish galleon,
with full sails,
moving towards me during my morning bath.
To touch you, is to find a worn creased map
that promises Ferdinand's ruby chest.
To feel your presence,
is to change all conversation,
as our words are changed under water.
Next time we meet,
let's keep our clothes on,
as nakedness symbolizes a kind of terrible innocence,
and my feelings for you have no innocence.
They are ancient, heavy, sexual, historic,
as a 100-year-old carp,
swimming in the moat
of some constantly besieged castle.

Love Poem to Francis X. Osgood

Love
is
a racket too,
and I
don't believe Robert Frost for one minute,
tho I love his poems.
                            Love, I said, is something
a motorcycle mechanic taught me about,
standing in bars,
looking into the mirror to see
whoever comes in
without looking at them.

I think of you
drinking my cognac,
looking in a mirror, knowing
I have no backhand,
not much forehand, and specialize in odd shots
when playing
close to the net.
I've never worked well with partners,
and yet I know that's one test
of strength.

I believe in all the new innovations,
including a different sized racket;
tennis is one of the few games
I can stand to watch.

Thinking of you,
burned out in L.A.
does not make me feel good. Love
is more important to give
than receive,
yet
this game reminds me
of reciprocity.

I hang out at tennis clubs, now,
in Detroit, Forest Hills, Connecticut and L.A.
Never seeing your name,
I know you are hitting the bourbon. But Francis,
that doesn't mean I've given up.

Meet me, some day,
on the terrace of the Beverly Wilshire.
I will not hand you a check and disappear. That's your fantasy,
not mine. For you were the one who wanted to dance
on European yachts. I
just went along
for the ride.

In tennis whites, I hail you /
disguised
as the lady jock
I never was.

For poems
are my only exercise.
And the net is always up
in my yard.

Francis,
I wait for you in every bar. Haunt every
tennis club. Want you to come
because
watching all those faces in the mirror
reminds me

57

of one face I look for.
And no matter what face I wake up with,
it is yours I see first,
like the ghost image of self, seen in the foggy shaving mirror
that I see
when I awaken, rosy and deep and morning sensuous;
no matter what different mustache
smiles and rallies
for the morning game.

The Fear of Dropping the Violin

Yes, M,
I look back, as I walk up the steps of the Greyhound
and see my friends with tears in their eyes,
but I do not see you
with yr Pancho Villa mustaches and big turquoise ring;
and the tears in my eyes are for many things more than parting
with friends.
Perhaps they are crying
because you are not here, either.
For my leaving is so common,
surely no one could cry over it.

Funny,
all my life I have talked of betrayers.
Those people who give you rings, gold rings, instead of themselves,

or those who never give you rings
or keys,
yet your keyring is heavy
like a jailer's, glittering with the secrets of oranges
and tropical birds.
And tonight, speeding along with the Greyhound under me, not
for the races,
only for life,
I realized that I was the betrayer
in the lives of many friends, many lovers even,
many
who needed me
and that I was always getting on a bus, or a plane,
sometimes even on a train
(in untrained America), or car.
Leaving,
not going away. Simply going somewhere else. Not because
I wanted to leave behind Laguna Beach, where the King of Spain
walked
every morning with sandpipers and gulls,
or George Washington in New York, thinking of plans for growing
European
laurel at Mt. Vernon when he came home from the ragged frozen
feet of Valley Forge,
or David who left me, sailing off a cliff into the ocean,
or Daniel who chased dream lions into the theater of his mind,
or the truckdriver, motorcycle mechanic, woodsman,
astronomer or dean.

Like a battleship,
my life goes on. Seen from an aerial view,
slow-moving, bulky and visible. It moves.
From the ground, what you see is me, moving with it,
not glinting as the gull above sees the quick scales of a fish,
but solid and black, as Barenboim's four-year-old piano.
Being loaded onto planes, buses, trains,
trucks,
or the battleships of life.

Like fire.
Like water.
Motion.
Constant motion. But not because there is some-
place
special
to go. The motion of life.
The keys of the piano, waiting for the willing hands to strike chords,
coax Beethoven and Chopin alike,
the keys moving in a world full of brilliant pianists,
and I,
the hammers, strings, keys, shining ebony of the heavy wood.
Play me,
play me, I say, and I will not betray you.
Do not be afraid of dropping me; I am not small.
Delicate and needing care, tuning, the skillful hands of loving
    pianists,
yes,
but not fragile,
not easily dropped,
even by an easily stage-frightened three-year-old
performer.

The Pepper Plant

for Bonnie

One word can
refer
to such
divergent
things.

> *Mabel, Mabel, set the table,*
> *And don't forget the red hot peppers.*
> —Children's Jump Rope Jingle

The sun rose
the color of a ripe red bell pepper.
The sun rose
the perfect shape and color of a Sumatran pepper berry.
I once saw the moon,
orange as a lantern,
rise in the winter sky.
                        It was the perfect shape
and color of a pepper berry.

The plant sits in our autumn patio,
glowing in the fog,
as if this were a New England wood,
and not a Southern California beach.
It is a pepper plant.
Sweet pepper.
Sometimes called bell or *garden.*
Many people do not know that red bell peppers are simply mature
    green

bell peppers.
But that's so,
and accounts for the red being
sweeter
and costing twice as much per lb.
in the super market.

The plant sitting in
our patio
is a sad one,
for it has no leaves or vine,
only the stick of its trunk,
and only the one fruit which ever grew on it,
a two-inch pepper, crimson but for one patch of green that is
actually
a scorched kind of black.
That pepper has been there for
almost three months.
It is now hardened,
glossy,
somewhat like a gourd,
too firm to eat,
(probably tasting like wood anyway).
It is like the one scarlet autumn
leaf
which hangs on a maple,
when all the other leaves are gone.

An image
of hardness,
or fool-hardiness?
Considering the pepper has no particular meaning
except perhaps to a poet
(substitute the word, "dreamer,"
or "idler")
who wants to see some beauty,
thus meaning,
in an object which just hangs on.

When I say the word, "pepper"
I actually don't think of a bell pepper,
I think
of that member of the genus *piper*
the hot black spice I put on everything
I eat.
That plant which grows in the tropics
"minute flowers clustered on catkin-like spikes"
and think of yr life which never has
enough peppery spice for you.

My husband, yr best friend, nearly
left me this week.
I guess I should say,
he did leave me. But came back.
Some mercy for which I do not know whom to thank—
Perhaps he left because I failed to give him
what he needs,
perhaps
because I am a failed person.
Irrelevant why.

My biggest struggle has been to find out why.
        Why I fear so much
        Why I feel so much
        Why I fail so much
        Why I keep trying
        Why I need to know so much.

And yet the absolute terror of life
is that there usually isn't a
reason why,
at least in any sense that you or anyone
could do anything about.
The frustration for us dreamer-doers.
That we cannot do anything about
the rain,
even though we dream and know it will come.
To provide for a rainy day means to wear a raincoat.

I once knew a girl who wore a raincoat everywhere; she was
considered eccentric, but it really was
that she was fat and ashamed of her figure. When it rained,
she got just as wet as the rest of us.
No one can prevent the rain.
Even Reich could not prevent the rain with orgone energy;
he only learned to make it;
occasionally to move it elsewhere.

In this library, where I'm sitting,
an old man is groaning over the atlas.
A girl with feminine accoutrements,
like
long blond hair,
large breasts,
a thin waist,
has just sat down at a neighboring table,
and she looks to me so much like a man, I keep looking over to
decide why.
Feminine hands and feet.
Woman's figure.
No sideburns.
Could it be that she has a man's face?
Her face has a thin straight nose,
fine lips;
intelligent look in her eyes.
This could be a description of my face.
Why do I see her as a man?

My thoughts wander.
For the past two days,
I have been in terror.
I have shivered. My teeth chattered.
I did not see or talk to anyone.
I read and slept.
Two normal activities which are important to me.
And tried to cut off my feelings
of anger at myself
that somehow

I could find myself at 37 trapped
into the same old dilemma;
me,
happy;
my husband,
miserable.
And he leaving (it is the only thing which
could transform my life with true misery now).

Hasty action seems to be
the ordinary answer to
misery.
And the miserable ones are the ones who have suffered too long.

Bonnie, you spent a year hating your children
and decided to move 3,000 miles
to change your life.
But, of course, you had to take
your children with you.
Yet, you are right about one thing:
you love your children more
than you hate them,
and what you really want
is not to have to spend all day
with them.
A simple request it would seem. But, I guess
not simple for any mother.

I think you wanted children for the same reason you say you
want to write poetry. A good reason. To transform your life.
And yet it is action, not object, which transforms a life. I could
have a Rembrandt painting hanging in my living room, and it
could not transform me; thus my life. But if I were painting a
picture because I loved the process of making that object, surely I
would then have a very different life? The process itself provides
much of the joy. So, your children, as objects, are no particular
joy to you alone—only when you can show them off (your
Rembrandt?) and to whom do you show off a constantly crying
baby? And your poetry? It gives you little joy, for no one reads

or publishes it. As an object, it is like your crying baby. Not much to show off.

It is ironic, of course, that the most beautiful objects are the ones produced by the artisan in love with his process, his craft, caring more for the process of making than for what will happen to the end result. It is only a bonus for some mothers that their children are prizes. The joy being in the human act of creating and living with them.

It is the daily process of living with my husband, being with him, that gives me joy. The only thing that can hurt me is to have that process taken away, to have his presence removed from my life. Whatever problems there are when he's there seem very possible to solve, since the process of life is to solve problems. The object, I suppose, of our lives is to be fulfilled by the process of living that life.

It occurred to me recently that I have never had love "objects" in my life, because the process of a relationship is what makes it alive. I think that is why I have been able to form and experience so many deep relationships with men. Perhaps that is also why I have not held them. And yet I do not feel that it would contradict what I have just said to now say that I have felt like I died each time a man I loved left me, and that, by the artist's magic, I literally had to recreate myself, to be born again, to start all over in order to have any life.

I don't want to spend my life as a phoenix, though. The fact that I can recreate myself is established. I have been forced for too many years to repeat the same process. I feel ready to go beyond that now.

All this started as a meditation on the pepper plant you gave us this summer, and on the notion that one word can signify many different things.

I do not believe pain
should be as important

as it is /
as it has been in history.
But I have lived with so much of it,
I can easily be usurped by it.
The pain of my last two days
was so identical to the pain of my past
that I could only sit
very still,
could not speak,
for I have said many times
everything there is
to say
about pain.

That is a trap, you know,
to have such an order of experience
there can never
be anything new
to say
about it.
And the fact is
that words cannot alleviate the pain;
they can only
express it.

Now, I want something to alleviate it,
the pain.
Know of nothing.
Am reminded that I began this meditation
for a reason.
To visualize the stringy pepper
red and burning green,
hanging on and on
to its stalk,
bringing New England autumn,
America's most remarkable season
into the changeless landscape of Southern California,
reminding that the pepper's cause is
purposeless,

but somehow it clings to life
like the single trite leaf still on a maple
in dead winter;

that, trite-I, surely,
could not have less strength.

For, I too love hot pepper,
but am more like a garden or bell
or sweet.

And Living is
the process of resisting death.
No one is willing to save us from death
but ourselves.
It's not
the prosy question of "can";
it's the poetic question of being willing.

No one is willing to save us from death,
but ourselves.
In this Southern California climate,
our pepper may remain,
                inedible,
                unpropagating,
                not terribly beautiful.

An emblem.
For me.
I hope I can look at it
as one of my moons, fallen out of the sky,
blood red,
with the green-black bruise,
the thumbprint of whoever
plucked it
out of a different sky.

Empty Night, When You Hear
the Surf Pounding

Like the flow of traffic
in a busy city,
I hear the waves, coming in, going out.
Alone,
I think of men I love.
None of them loves me.
                              There is a beach in California,
where the King of Spain has rowed in
from his own country,
and were I in a certain house there,
listening to that surf, instead of the one I hear now
in my head, I would at least
feel him,
the man I could accept
like a lover of darkness who is not supposed to be seen,
even in candlelight, the one who would
disappear before even the veins of colour streak
dawn sky.

But here, alone, now,
in this room, full of the accoutrements of moonlight
and shooting stars, where mercury
is not a vaporlamp, but part of my fingertips,
I cannot deceive myself, even, with the possibility
of his presence.

My phone rang once before I went to bed,
but no one was on the line, either,
and then sleeping, I dreamed

that no one but me lived anywhere in this world. The mad Pole
loved a bar waitress—
The Librarian was chasing a black dancer—
The Woodsman had an art editor—
The Astronomer, a scholar of Jacobean drama—
oh heavens, who can list
all the men
who are not there when even the King of Spain
is in another state?

Empty night,
when you hear
the surf pounding,
mocks me
beyond even the solace of dawn.

III. Fifteen Poems for a
Lunar Eclipse
None of Us Saw

I. Not the Blood a Dreamer Kissed
from My Mouth

Wanting to make music
as if each note could be cut into shape;
as if an arm manipulated a shoulder and hand
and objects could come as clean
as ideas.

Wishing beauty were not owned.

Wanting a rose to be
more original.

And the moon not so old that it was
decaying tomato-red, soft mush
when my fingers clean out the vegetable
bin / the moon I put in there
firm, round; not the blood a dreamer kissed from my mouth.

II. The Dream

A dream / like a fire truck
with a dalmatian sitting
by the chief

> two men love me
> more than their own lives

> the arrow
> which was shot into my
> heart

> blood in my mouth
> thick as porridge

> and yet I did not feel
> as if I were dying

> one kisses the blood away
> from my mouth / his own
> face retains a smear
> what does the other one
> do? For I sense both of them
> as loving me.
> Yet only one holds me,
> cradles me, kisses
> the blood from my mouth.
> The other
> is only present.

I feel I am loved by two.
Yet only one
does the touching.

III. *Water*

yr element,
the ocean, a metallic plate
on which all the bread
in loaves as big
as whales
is cut.

    Scorpion's tail,
wet earth,
and desert sand

            cactus in the foot
like stars
sitting in the palms /
No diamonds fall
from fingers or toes.
Only your smile reminds me
it is water I love
and the shining creatures
which live in it

    sting ray
    manta
    dragon fish
    coral devils

even their housing
yielding
to water, that big
soft pressure.

IV. Write

a letter
once in a while," he said.
But words
would not come.
Black lines on paper
were symbols

      moons burnt out at the end of a hot night
      sun flowers with charred faces
      stars like old teeth
      which fell out of a rosy mouth

when words are more important than food,
being
the only reality,
the only tangible possibility
for survival,
they become the diamond dogs
rising and running
out from the ashes.

My letters would be terrible
in their insistence,
coming more often
than meteor showers,
                  but filling
the sky.
Obscuring the steady planets

and old constellations.
New suns, new galaxies,
but nothing that could be called
coming
        "once in a while."

V. For Michael, Armoured with Roses

Roses covered Lorca's breast.
Roses blossomed on my lover's hands.
Roses were in my own mouth instead of words.
All the blood drawn from history's thorns
could not transfuse life
where life does not want to be.
It is the fragrance,
the textures, I love most.
Only blind men need color. But, of course,
you know I am going blind.
                                    History.

VI. The Lady who Sang

Her name was written somewhere in cobwebs.
Her songs were written by spiders.
Sometimes the moon applauded
but mostly the moon slept
simple and quiet as porcelain.
She drank roses
and held thorns to protect the man she loved.
Michael rescued her
with a rope of pearls thrown down into the well
where she was drowning.
Lorca kissed her lips.
Someone threw emeralds over her feet
as she lay.
Her songs were filled with the snails
which climbed up the old well walls, and carp,
ancient fish, the small frogs
which shared their voices at night.

She is invisible
but Michael sees her.
The lady who sang
sings a song for only one man.

VII. The Dark Clack of Morays

> "A three foot Moray Eel, from the
> coastal waters of Lower California.
> Large specimens can inflict dangerous
> wounds with their strong jaws set with
> needle-sharp teeth."
>
> —World Book Encyclopedia

The dark clack of morays like dead leaves on the ground.

The dark clack of morays like dead leaves on the ground.

VIII. Light

The roses glowed in the room, and she wrote by rose light. Her
eyes were candles. Her fingers had diamonds in them for none to
see. Roses bloom in every place like snails in a rainy season.
Listen to me: light from roses is not unusual. Turn out all false
lights.

IX. Sun with Hands for Rays

You big sun
touching me like you own me
I will put rings on all
your fingers
weigh you down with
jasper and malachite.
You big sun
my lips are bloodstone
sardonyx.

And just wait till you see all the
bracelets.

X. Donna

Mary called them buttonflowers. I called them by the name of
stalky, worrywort, broadstraw. One name is never enough for
me, for I learned young that names are everything. Thus, many
names are many treasures.

One name:
a fortune,
or death.
Call me Diane,
moon,
silver archer,
huntress,
pillar of marble.

XI. The Roses were Talking

This time she was able to hear them
though she had been deaf all these years.
Her fingers were crystals.
The roses were talking.
But all they said was,
"Breaking, breaking,"
and some would have sworn it was the wind,
or just imagination.

I found that I wanted nothing
from people,
but their lives;
for poetry,
music,
even the roses
are the antithesis of labor.
When work is play
then it might become art.
The flowers will never tell you this.

XII. Eat your Rose Hips, c'est la vie

Once there was a spirit
who took the form of a poem.
However,
since poems in the 20th century
often seem formless,
this caused a great deal of trouble
for the spirit.

XIII. Poetry, the Unpredictable

You ask me questions
that I can answer.
They do not satisfy me,
like the pkgs of seeds sitting on my desk:
Anaheim sweet peppers and mammoth dill from Ferry-Morse
    Company,
seeds I may not even plant, and which surely have
very little chance of growing well for one who travels,
plants in pots, and then has to leave
the pots for others to tend.

My green thumb excites me
for there is no answer to why some things grow and others don't
and botany classes never really taught me why some plants have
    buds and
others don't.

I only know that roses excite me
and other growing things.
And the ocean at my door, behind my windows,
in these fingers;
that is a sound.
I love it / yet it frightens me at night.

The unknown,
the mysterious,
those of us who need to know
everything, find that
the more we know,

the more things we don't know
excite us.

Poetry?
Surely the most unpredictable?
Like the roses
of our landlord's
which did not get eaten
by worms.

XIV. David

There is a swirling scribble
in my desk's blotter
which looks like a fingerprint
from some large hand.

I know its source
(a pen which would not write,
my hand's firm pressure engraving
the spiral lines into the soft green face)
yet looking
just now
I thought perhaps
it was you, David,
who had returned.
My brother,
dead all these years.

XV. Western Music

I don't want to be
a fool about this: but the moon seemed to be floating
on the ocean this morning,
early
before I awoke,
before I walked down to see
that watery surface
I could not survive in.

Why do I remember this,
living in a rain forest, where snails and slugs
try to invade the bathroom,
where the shower is growing pale green orchids,
and where Michael's hand often
has mushrooms
sprouting on the knuckles?

Surely salt
kills moon creatures.
The pillar
a mirage
in the desert. Rain
only a rhyme
from a french form,
the tonic chord
in this Western music.

IV. Those Mythical Silver Pears

Those Mythical Silver Pears

for Steve

I remember a past
of playing Beethoven sonatas
in a dark house over the water,
and lights from the hills surrounding me
instead of the arms of the man I love.

You remember playing
basketball,
tall, Egyptian, silent,
a stone figure,
no one ever talked to.

Neither of us
ever lived outside our own heads,
you trying to do what you thought others expected,
I trying to coax love out of the keyboard,
you throwing baskets
where there was no hoop,
I imagining a music no one could hear.

We sit together in your kitchen
which is dark,
not full of the life of someone who cooks,
a photograph kitchen,
I drinking
with my feet up on the chairs, the way I like
to sit, and thinking of the girls

next door, in the other lighted kitchen,
the ones who must think you are handsome, who idealize
tall men,
who have gone to basketball games and cheered,
though they never saw you there then.

This is the painful story of two imaginary people,
living like lions in their heads,
but the world sees them as Sphinx,
silent,
locked into mineral,
surrounded by desert and night.

Women fantasize a life of love that cannot exist.
Men, the competition of games and seduction of crowds.
We set up a world no one can question:
the past,
our private diaries.

If we were sitting in your kitchen eating, right now,
you would be drinking a glass of
mercury.
And I, biting
into one of those mythical silver pears.

A Broken Season

for Jim

When I am 55
and you 43
and we both find ourselves slightly
nostalgic,
when passion has not deserted us,
but gone underground
like ants,
leaving little hills of fine dirt
above the entrance holes
as a reminder of past work,
maybe we
will meet
in some bar,
perhaps
in Wyoming,
smiling at each other,
maybe touching once,
                    out of some required discretion,
and you will inquire about
my husband,
and I, about your beautiful wife,
and we will mumble assurances
of their health
and pleasure,
knowing such things are important
irrelevancies,
and like the ants

we will continue carrying our mouthful
of fine earth,
words about the mountains and poetry and loyalty
and the craft of building.

When,
20 years from now,
we live
just as we do now,
separately,
even our letters coming only in a broken season,
times between lovers or jobs or invention,
we might indulge once
in a statement like,
"love only happens once,
and it never works out,"
and then

smile at our own sentimentality.

The ants travel in long strings, like your daughters'
hair ribbons, carry
loads of sweet cake or the bodies of
maggots down into their tunnels.
They build and eat,
zig-zagging around obstacles in their paths.

Children watch them in school.
We tread them underfoot.
Small mammals eat them.
I cannot imagine a future
any different
from the past.

Saying Goodby to Someone You were just Getting Ready to Say Hello To

I chased you thru Michigan
as if you were a whooping crane
going extinct.
                    And I drove thru
bloody maples
while California wrapped its tourniquet of palm trees
around my scarred arms,
reminding me of times when the blood gushed out
and filled the street in a pool.

And finally, I caught you
by telephone line, discovering I could not put salt on
your tail.
For my mother,
that well of bad information,
had told me as a child that
salt on the tail
was traditional means of catching birds.
                    But you,
no whooping crane,
a fish instead, whose shimmering body,
like a salmon, seen black against the white of the falls as
it jumps uselessly, trying to get over,
                    you
were the one fish whose energy (thank you, Elizabeth Bishop)
would inspire me to loose the hook, throw you back
in the water.

I search now for truck drivers in baby blue semis,
shifting gears into Lorca and Stevens,
or long distance runners who will give me a fast chase,
the Woodsmen who disappear into Saskatchewan where the woods are
too tangled for me to come through.
I still listen to the poetry of dewpoints on the news of my
childhood radio, wondering about citrus ranchers or
cattlemen.

Alone, at night, I wash my crystal,
listen to Debussy,
drink a 1970 red bordeaux,
and write letters.

It is not just American, but
a worldly gesture
to be interested in the rare birds,
those going extinct.
I visited the land of the whooping cranes once.
Never saw any of them, tho.
And I will miss you now
like any extinct creature.
Like some natural part of the landscape
replaced by fossil and footprint.

The Skier

for M. B.

Squinting eyes
against the hilly snow,
you are red-gold and thin enough in
the hips to bend like the tail of a lizard,
the cold winter full sun
lighting you up in my mind.

You stand,
battered and beat up
from a day on the slopes
in your down parka
at the end of a bar, full of faces like camomile flowers in a bare field,
drinking bourbon.

Girls eye you,
as if you are the last piece of devil's food cake,
knowing your body is hard and fresh from the snow,
tingling in the knees and hips,
flakes frosting your eyelashes.
They watch the slope of your shoulders,
as you turn away from the bar,
thinking of the winter hills.
They know you are ready
to take one of them to bed and
to move all over their own bodies, as
white slopes,
small hills, powdered mountains,

sliding icily,
                    flushed burning with the heat
of dry ice.

I, non-
athlete,
non-skier or swimmer,
warm singer of icy chants,
I watch you
and talk with you
and, when I dare—
                    touch you,
knowing,
for an instant,
about this cool sport;

but I was born with inner-ear upsets,
have only an odd grace
that stumbles
with no real sense of balance.
Skiing would exhilarate me for one minute
and surely kill me
the next.
I have none. No sense
of balance.
I could scream with pleasure
in that first rush down a simple white hill
and then in an instant
hit a tree or twist my bones,
breaking hips that are already brittle,
cracking my back or neck like a chicken,
those parts of me which always give dull pain
in any weather.

Yes, I liked hearing
about you,
and surely desired you
more than you could ever have wanted me.

But I am smart enough to know
I am no skiier,
that you could not love a stumbler
on the slopes,
that I could not ever give myself
wholly to
any sport,
              save perhaps one . . .

Hello there,
beautiful skiier,
I am here alone,
in a dark house,
watching snow fall over winter hawthorne and elm,
thinking of this wintery world,
—how
              I like looking out of
the windows at it,
thinking,
not touching,
knowing the pain of too many
cold failures.

Loving you,
thin, red-gold,
with all your other girls,
for your natural,
deadly,
athletic,
American
wintery
success.

Dear Michael,

here's a poem for you,

Marriage Poem

the pocketbook plant
whose red-orange flowers have speckled lips
sits on our table
and reminds me of you,
who makes love to me,
                    yr bare shoulders
rising out of winter blankets
freckled brown against the white

my own body,
                    soft and winter-pure

I wd wear an opal
like a hen's egg glowing at my throat
a thin thread of ribbon
that separates my words from yrs

we are lovers,
house plants, vermillion calceolaria or purple crocus,
colors against winter
that loneliness
which now lives only
back of our eyes sometimes,
in the thin wire around yr little finger,
on my lips which braid history
a few books now getting dusty
on our busy shelves.

The Wandering Tattler

for Michael

grey
against the rocks
like the cardboard in back of a sheaf
of typing paper,
the wandering tattler
searching for soft wet food
in tide pools and muscle beds
bobs,
splashes,
disappears into jagged crevices . . .

What are we looking for?
A chance to name
living things?
A metaphor for love?
Words against
the continuous process,
like starfish,
bruised purple, the red of paprika, yellow
like nasturtiums,
spreading in off-rhyme,
the alliteration of membrane,
ocean a symbol,
rock a metaphor,
the grey bird an image moving in this

landscape?

I love you.
Walked through this world with you
yesterday;
last night;
this morning.

Harry Moon from my Child's
Anthology of Verse

People want to create themselves
as characters,
as the principal actors in their own . . .

                                no, I will not say
"drama."
           Wisdom, no, that is not the word either;
           age? maturity? vision? sensibility?
           something begins to give the unspoken,
           the unnamed more credibility;
           silence becomes the only rejoinder.

He said, of himself,
           "It was raining,
           and Harry was walking barefoot.
           With his dog.
           Just a boy and his dog in the rain."

My husband said,
           "That day it was raining—
           I was walking on the beach
           and I saw a man dressed in a black suit
           with a white shirt and narrow black tie.
           I thought it was Nixon walking on the beach
           in the rain."

I said
        nothing.
Thinking of a girl, riding naked on her zebra,
wearing only her diamonds.

107

Saturn,
The planet of silence.
Its rings of broken rock. Rocky silence.
Circle me.
Marry my lips to each other.

I was once the moon,
a small body causing the tides.

                              Names,

are
accidental.

                    I could not say
I was a girl riding naked on a zebra,
wearing only her diamonds.
So I remained silent.
I was looking out the window
seeing the roses and poppies hemorrhaging against my eyes
a yellow orchid plant, trailing old lace,
and knowing my beautiful ocean
was a block away. Why should anyone care?
Yet
I was touched that Harry Moon saw himself as the
simple American image,
a boy walking barefoot in the rain with his dog.
The perfect audience
is composed of people who no longer want to be on stage.
I was wishing somehow,
that I could become part of the landscape
(for I love principally the ideas of things).

*   *   *

Harry Moon

"The moon's the North Wind's cookie,
He eats it day by day"
                    —Christopher Morley

It was a promise of self that made him
come to work each day. And I wonder if
the scarlet roses and poppies I saw
hemorrhaging themselves against my eyes
when I walked through the morning lawn had shocked
me? As if they were the overtures
to a musical program: my day.

Yet drama, not music, was the morning's substance,
and I was stunned (sleepy), the perfect audience.
He said,
arranging our chairs,
          "It was raining, and there Harry was,
              barefoot, walking alone with his dog."

The sun was shining this morning as Harry
Moon recited the entire drama of himself
in those two lines.
A poetic image, the amazing drama of
self-portrait, creating a self for others
he does not think we would ourselves
perceive.
              This language of yellow orchid plants,
trailing their lace, of pink stucco houses
and palm trees, Mercedes driving on freeways,
and Spanish arches under terra cotta tiles
moves me now, as music once moved me;
that is, it awes, terrifies me, so that
I want to freeze it, hold it there, not
in memory or the mind's eye,
for aging cells hold only imperfect images,
but truly, perhaps as in a painting.

I once thought I was the moon.
Named Diane, I fought all day with the sun
which was trying so hard to obscure me.
But now I see the daytime invisible moon
as a comfortable reality. I now am afraid
of the sun's departure, leaving me radiant

and alone to be watched in the sky.
Harry Moon presented himself to me
this morning at the improbable cottage.
He was from my own child's anthology of verse,
Silver Pennies. I look for a country now
where silver pennies are the coinage and the people
are generous actors, sharing their own perfect
visions of themselves. But the newspapers
never reveal diamonds.

I wanted to say that I was out, also in the rain—
you all understand that it rained here yesterday, tho
the sun is shining now?—
riding naked on my zebra, wearing only
my diamonds. But I could not;
for it was a vision that rescued me
when I had nothing in my life but dust.
And yesterday, I was sitting by my fireplace,
reading in peace.

My husband said to Harry Moon,
        "I was out walking on the beach in the rain
        and I saw a man also walking on the beach,
        wearing a black suit and a white shirt with a
        narrow black tie. I thought it was Nixon."

Eagles were flying in the air above the cottage then.
I was not out in the rain yesterday,
creating a role for myself. I hated diamonds for many years,
as I cried all the time, and in my fairy tale world
the tears became diamonds, which I wore around my neck,
on my fingers, wrists and toes.
Crystal fragments of my pain,
cold, stunning.
Now I wish I had real diamonds.
After you hate something many years
you grow to love it for itself.

*   *   *

Harry Moon

"The moon walks alone
in her silver shoon."
—John Masefield

Sprays of baby's breath on the table
reminded of the ocean, a block away,
and the scarlet roses and poppies on the lawn
hemorrhaged against my eyes. Sharp knives
of unfolded Bird of Paradise cut
into morning,
as Harry Moon said,
from out of the context of poetry,
      "It was raining and Harry was out
      walking barefoot in the rain with
      his dog."
My husband replied,
      "I was out walking on the beach in the rain
      and I saw a man also walking on the beach
      wearing a black suit with a white shirt and
      narrow black tie. I thought it was Nixon."
In my own mind, I knew
that I savoured
in my own mind
the *idea* of walking on the beach,
barefoot in the rain,
but actually I was sitting by the fire,
savouring in my mind
a girl riding naked on her zebra,
in the rain,
wearing only her diamonds.
In the rain the diamonds did not show.
Rock and drop were unities.
Saturn is a planet
surrounded by rings made of diamonds.
It is called the marriage planet.

As we sat by our table in the cottage
eating breakfast a block from the sea,
I kept seeing silver pennies falling
on the floor around me. I worried
like David Ignatow about whether anyone else
saw them.
The silver coins piling higher and higher around my rocky ankles
and knees.

If I do not speak to you,
it is the mounds of silver pennies which I hear clinking near
my lips and throat.
Harry Moon, from my childhood anthology of poetry,
knows that silence
can be part of a dialogue too.

Polish Love Poem for Dan whose Last Name is Harder to Pronounce than Mine

The "M" on my arm
stands for
moon.
And you are another one of those men who drive well,
making me feel
(as I sit in yr car / speeding over the state of Michigan)
that
Movement
is what my life stands for.

Yet how often the moon has slipped out of my fingers
like a glass shade smashing to the floor.

My friends hold me well.
But you make me rise from the chair, the bed.
Move towards you.
Move with you.

Don't let too many girls paint lightning
over yr eyes.
"M" also stands for murder.
And marriage.

Movements away,
as well as towards.

Love, the Lizard

I read some love letters
by the man I love.
But they were not written to me.
My feelings were silent
as lizards on the desert.

Some say that when flowers are torn out of the ground
they can cry.
If so,
it must be a secret language,
a quiet one;
I wish I could speak it to you
and tell you of all the hurts I have endured
and yet come through,
unwilling to give up,
or mentally die,
willing to spend my life with you—
          difficult and moody as you are,
               even tho yr love letters are to other women.
Like a lizard,
you disappear silently
over yr own wall.

Silence is something
I do not trust
any more.
We all must speak
and finally
live by our own words.

The Tattooed Man who Swallows Swords

Rejection is an infinite dialogue,
a landscape that does not end,
not a forest, or a field, for those places have boundaries,
or even an ocean, with its beach,
like a necklace of scars.

And acceptance,
simple act,
a territory with limitations.
It took me years
to want to explore a territory
if I knew it had a border,
the confines being my beginning place,
I walking from the outer extent, even farther out.

Once when I was walking in a place I thought
was new unboundaried land,
I met a man with a hammer and saw;
he had tigers tattooed all over his body; they
stalked his belly and shoulders while he worked
at a carpenter's bench.
I stopped to watch him build a small cabinet.
My body was covered with bells,
like a skin of silver balls which covered everything
but my nipples which protruded, small and pink, as coral.

When I moved, I jangled softly,
as if my hair was a curtain of beads for a doorway
and someone entered brushing the curtain aside.

I said,
    "I envy carpenters for the things they make
        with their hands."
"Yes," he said,
"but I am only a beginner. What I really do well
is to swallow swords."

Then I opened my throat and showed him
a green snake which lived inside;
I said,
    "We are strangers,
        but we both have something in common,
        we both walk in the places beyond boundary,
        and now I see we both have throats which can contain
        what most men fear,
        what they think they would die of,
        the snake and the sword."

Life is often more allegorical
than it should be;
in life, stories do not have endings
but are continuations, hiatuses,
not stories, but continual dialogue in the mind.
I will not make a story where none occurs.

Once upon a time,
I said, "I love you," and found my tongue burned out at the root,
and now I have a sleek green snake which lives there,
and hisses out when you walk by.
You swallowed swords until your throat was thick with scars,
so thick a sword would no longer go down.

And here is the scene,
not a story,
but a landscape.
I, standing in the forest, my body shivering with bells,
and a snake hissing like waterfalls in my throat,
you in front of me,
tattooed with tigers that move across your shoulders

and around your ears,
as your hands construct a handsome piece of furniture
and your perfect throat
seen from the outside
also squeezes vowels that will not come out,
even the membrane of language not thin enough to slip through
those old swollen tissues.

V. Recognizing that My Wrists always have Salmon Leaping for Spring in Them

Recognizing that My Wrists always have Salmon Leaping for Spring in Them

for Jason

"Betrayal?"
              he asked me / the
one word ending
in a questionmark.
What *do*
I mean by that?
Surely not
simply
that someone could not do what I expected of him?
As,
there are no strings attached to love,
no rights or reasons to expect others to feel
as you do.
              It was a cold February,
              wet, snowy streets,
              fire burning in the fireplace & cognac
              spilling across our throats,
              my mind was a dogsled to the arctic,
              my wrists had salmon leaping for spring in them,
              I could always return
              to fire & ice,
              but would the barking dogs drown out
              the splashes in my pulse?

No,
no,
betrayal is not so simple—

a breach of faith,
an abandonment of loyalty,
a promise broken,
implying that
first
the promise had been made.

And I aching for the mechanic,
the man who rides motorcycles through the dusty craters
of the moon,
                    races with the sun,
                                    wearing salmon bones around his neck,
who left me for trees he will cut down,
& a pond which seeped away last spring,
thinking of my hands
against the body & face of the arctic
which is my life
the fire
in that stone fireplace burning—
        what?
images of myself as false expector.

I tried to talk of betrayal
but could only think
of how impossible
yet necessary it is
for us to expect ANYTHING
from other human beings.
The question
pulled my mind very fast,
the runners of the dogsled skidding
over years of snow.
In my wrists
the salmon return every spring
and lay their shining eggs.
We are faithful always
to ourselves,
those leapings and slidings which take us

somewhere
we feel
we must go.

A Poem for the Man who Drives the Sphinx and Makes All Ferrari Owners Weep with Envy

You are always speeding
on cat's paws
down desert roads.
                    Yr girls
have transparent coats
made of raindrops:
sweet and naked, they
disappear
into the desert
and return with cinnamon
dusting their lips and ankles.
They send you messages
inside Arab-scented cardamom
seeds.

I sit in admiration,
loving mechanics and drivers of
good machines,
knowing that ancient vehicles
are often the most elegant,
wondering how many strange & beautiful
neighbors
I will discover
over the years,
living in the Egyptian desert.

For a long time now,
I've gambled with the tarot,
and ridden my okapi, naked,

galloping past Tanzania
into working men's bars where
all lovers are poets,
and diamonds betray their owners,
where hope is an ocean shark,
and temptation, a myth.

This note is to welcome you to my
neighborhood,
to say what a pleasure it is to see you
speeding along,
driving the sphinx,
to say I hope you like this country,
to offer you an invitation
to stop off whenever passing
and have a drink /
from this ocean,
our poetry.

Bracelets

The quiet girl / her silver face tilted to the firelight
turns the room into a forge.
The night burns light,
the Bethlehem Steel plant,
and my ankle protruding from the
compactness of my chair-body,
seems burnished, for it is summer.

Presence
surely created
an ancient form of deity.
Vulcan was ugly from the waist down / he
worked with magnificent bronzed-statue arms.
His wife
had power
over us all.
I am the voyeur /
whoever I watch
is a slave. As you sit in firelight
I see glinting
the bracelets
that clasp your ankles,
that slide on your wrists. Chains are
decorations
in the mean eye
of the jailor.

On the Subject of Roses

California shakes its petals / poppies
are lying against the hills,
orange in their careless motion,
like goldfish swimming in and out
of an aquarium castle.

Bad music
gives a bad life. But no one
should have to choose between Mozart and Beethoven.
Yes,
a brilliant day is
necessarily
one with flowers.

No, Mozart
and Beethoven
were not rivals.

What the Struggle is All About

for poets, who are always alone

Walking
on a crowded street today
I saw an interesting-
looking
      man
say,
to a boring-looking woman,

                "Do you have the keys, honey?"

A blister on
my foot,
from walking on keys,
a scar on my arm where the key I sleep on
gouges into me,
a lump in my throat where the key sticks,
scratches across my belly where someone tried to force keys
into locks, improperly,
a hand which is five bone keys
locking the doors to pain,
locking me against a world I love but do not trust;
and I walked down the street jangling with keys,
jangling with anger
at my life, and the iron door which locks it against the world,
a past unlocked with a skeleton key,
Saturn, my husband,
dark and foreboding,
a mean old man, silent and desperate with time,

128

locking me against all that I desire,
                    smiling,
                         she says,
                              "No,
I gave them to you,
honey."
and he digging into his pockets,
finds them,
also smiles.
I stop
at the seaside bar,
alone,
have my drink,
watch everyone
watching me,
behind my iron gate,
locked tight,
no questions of where the key is,
no questions.
          "Private"
          "No Trespassing"
          "Posted"
I drink my drink.
Let
    my mind wander.
It has no locks,
no keys,
no guards,
no bars.
Except the one I drink at.
The fountain of life.

Some Man

You are not
Beethoven.
You are not
anything like
George Washington.
You have no diamonds
to scratch me with,

                    but I am a hard diamond myself / try
to cut me any
other way.

When I go walking on the beach
at sunset,
and the ocean
is gossiping about death,
I see the print
of your bootheels
somewhere ahead of me,
hear the sounds of leather, as you walk towards me,
the dowitchers, sandpipers and gulls
ignore our shadows
which are only part of the sunset.

                              A blvd. of movie-
stars.
This world we dream from.

Hello, Man,
I say,
knowning there is an "M" carved deeply

into one of my arms.
Flashing the silver on your little finger,
twirling your mustache,
your boots leaving deep wedges in the sand,
you pass me.
                    I,
                    wondering where
                                    you are going.

My hair is flying.
There are silver fish in the sea.
I wonder if
I am invisible
                tho my voice
                        has landed on the sand like a sardine.
Gasping for air.

There is no turning.
No real talking.
Because neither of us
is real.
You,
flashing boots,
dark mustache,
a silver ring;   I,
a girl. Any girl.

Take a girl,
Any girl.

Pick a card,
any card.

The Old Golden Fleece

for J. A.

You smoke
too much, I sd,
doesn't it make you feel bad
when you wake up
in the morn-
ings?

No, he sd. I'm not on
one of those purity trips
you poets
all seem to take.

Taking out a pack of filter
cigarettes, he
shook one out into
his palm,
poked it into his mouth.
Gotta match, he sd.

I handed him
a book. His hand
was shaking.
I thot maybe he was a tiger.
I was lost in the sun
(sunshine).
I could not sail a ship.
I could not play the piano.
I was never going to be a tennis pro.

When I saw something
I wanted,
like a tiger or lion,
or perhaps something small
like a snail or
sea urchin,
I would ask for it.
But,
there was no use telling
him anything.
He was just one of those smokers.
One of those guys
lost in their own cloud.

in the palm

of,

in the palm OF
     IN
the palm of your hand

I am
in the palm of yr
hand

I am in
the palm of yr
hand.
A line.
A hard line.

In the palm of your strong hand.

VI. Daughter Moon

Daughter Moon

for P. R.

(Strega.
Witch.
Broken line of contact.)

I imagine you as Penelope
in the version of the story which gives her
power over dark seduction.

The weaving and unweaving
leaves you free to remove yourself magically
each night to a shrine of eucalyptus.
The moon's glittering footprints
make snail tracings
through the grove.
You move towards the mysteries
women preserve—
all of us who have slept with warring,
travelling, unfaithful men,
and whose bodies have split open
with the blood of childbirth,
the labor of spewing   a man
covered with cheesey slippery birth
into the world.
After love,
after parturition,
after the agony,
of splitting off a piece of the crater

of your body
you move away from
the bed. Walk to the grove at night
where Hecate
takes your dark head in her hands;
the silence of women.

You wear long silver materials,
stand liquid before an altar
of all the late dawns you have endured alone;
betrayals are the branches
of deciduous fir, moving like moths
against your face.
The moon is a solid light,
a silver coin you can never spend.
You are alone
in a black and silver world;
worship
is only your eyes beginning to adjust themselves
to see in the dark.

Marriage,
possession,
sharing a remaining bed with an insistent husband,
is a struggling fish,
drops of water have flashed out and away from your struggle
—which one are you?
                    The fisherman / woman,
the powerful muscle of delicate flesh?

I see you still alone in the grove,
understanding at last
the interchangability of men,
the sons split out of your body,
the wandering husband whose place
you save in bed with your unravelling tapestry,
and now the lovers who follow you secretly
to the grove,
for a secret mating,

and arrive too early,
finding you magically there touching
something so simple
which terrifies the not-woman.

Tonight I had my portion of strega
and thought of you, whom I will probably never know,
imagined this grove
where you walk in the silvery illumination
of my grey (like the flat ocean) eyes.
Slept
and arose at dawn.
                    Silver, silver,
time.

A daughter of the silver moon.
No wonder,
she,
you,
I,
love that golden invisible man.
The King of Spain.
The wearer of the Cap of Darkness.
Whose light is mysterious.
Only shown to the women slipping down
soft silver stairways
of themselves.

Two

trees
stand
outside this
window.
       Inside
this room
is the ocean,
all the salt
that ever was,
a big rock,
a mtn,
a beach,
the eye of 9 beholders,
greed,
and sorrow,
the drama of the piney needles.

Ode to a Lebanese Crock of Olives

for Walter's Aunt Libby's
diligence in making olives

As some women love jewels
and drape themselves with ropes of pearls, stud their ears
with diamonds, band themselves with heavy gold,
have emeralds on their fingers or
opals on white bosoms,
I live with the still life
of grapes whose skins frost over with the sugar forming inside,
hard apples, and delicate pears;
cheeses,
from the sharp fontina, to icy bleu,
the aromatic chevres, boursault, boursin, a litany of
thick bread, dark wines,
pasta with garlic,
soups full of potato and onion;
and butter and cream,
like the skins of beautiful women, are on my sideboard.

These words are to say thank you
to
Walter's Aunt Libby
for her wonderful olives;
oily green knobs in lemon
that I add to the feast when they get here from Lebanon
(where men are fighting, as her sisters have been fighting
for years, over whose house the company stays in)
and whose recipes for kibbee or dolmas or houmas
are passed along.

I often wonder,
had I been born beautiful,
a Venus on the California seashore,
if I'd have learned to eat and drink so well?
For, with humming birds outside my kitchen window to remind
     of small elegance,
and mourning doves in the pines & cedar, speaking with grace,
and the beautiful bodies
of lean blond surfers,
dancing on terraces,
surely had I a beautiful face or elegant body,
surely I would not have found such pleasure
in food?
I often wonder why a poem to me
is so much more like a piece of bread and butter
than like a sapphire?
But with mockers flying in and out of orange groves,
and brown pelicans dipping into the Pacific,
looking at camelias and fuchsia,
an abundance of rose, and the brilliant purple ice plant
which lined the cliffs to the beach,
life was a "Still Life" for me.
And a feast.
I wish I'd known then
the paintings of Rubens or David,
where beauty was not only
thin, tan, California girls,
but included all abundance.

As some women love jewels,
I love the jewels of life.
And were you,
the man I love,
to cover me (naked) with diamonds,
I would accept them too.

Beauty is everywhere,
in contrasts and unities.
But to you, I could not offer the thin tan fashionable body

of a California beach girl.
Instead, I could give the richness of burgundy,
dark brown gravies,
gleaming onions,
the gold of lemons,
and some of Walter's Aunt Libby's wonderful olives from Lebanon.

Thank you, Aunt Libby,
from a failed beach girl,
out of the West.

To the Thin and Elegant Woman who Resides Inside of Alix Nelson

Curly-head,
plump little mother's girl,
like a delicious peach in August,
and now yr pit wants to burst out
into a Vogue model with peacock eyes and slinky hips that
are like swan-necks, even in the bulky clothes from Autumn Saks,
this is an invocation to dump
fashion,
to love your own soft peachy cheeks,
to show your white arms like sweet pillows
and to let men be lovers,
not faggots.
           (Oh, yes, Thom Gunn, who protested that word in the
New York Review of Books,
I *will* use it.)
For now is the time to proclaim
                 men AND
women
as lovers; and to proclaim
our own Rich
American bodies,
filled with healthy vegetables,
and marbled Charolais meat,
the rich red wines of France,
and the stinging white ones from California.

Now is the time to love flesh, for once a country has produced
flesh that it does not deny or destroy,

civilization has come a long way, baby.
Every sophomore writes poetry. And every truckdriver watches
     Bertolucci.
Every housewife plays the harpsichord,
and most businessmen know philosophy and chess. So,
                                                  how
can we live with these punishing ideas,
that a woman with a boy's body is beautiful, till she has to starve
herself on rye-thins and non-fat cottage cheese. How can my husband
with his Pancho Villa mustaches and divorce papers in briefcase
put bells on his pants and work out at Vic Tanney's while taking off
his wedding ring, trying,
trying,
like all of you,
to be slim.

A critic of life sent me a letter this week, denouncing my thin lips,
and the life of constant movement. But I am like water
or fire,
never still. Yet, she has never
seen me.
My sturdy Polish, German, American body, filled with sausage
and cheese and wine, always sharp from the vinegar of salads
     and pickles
and spicy from the hot food I also love. Love is
substantial.
Love, I say,
is sturdy and lasts longer than anything else.
She complains of my thin veneer,
but I am a new painting,
not an old one.

Allow me my American prerogatives, I say.
Forget faggots and their thin bodies.
The confusion of Pentimento.
Clarity: like Goethe,
I want more light, more clarity, more vision.
And I think of my California landscape,

145

the thin palm trees on their pencil-like stalks, which are imports.
The fat stubby palms, which are native to the landscape.

And I will not diet on toast and lettuce, for my lettuce is
leafy and fresh, from endive to chicory, with cilentro and cress,
and tossed with crumbled roquefort, thick fresh olive oil from
the Mediterranean and vinegar aromatic with tarragon.
My body is full of the juice of poetry.
I am not even thin from lack of love, for perhaps what I have
learned is that Americans,
we, have so much, we all love too much,
or, perhaps, better stated, not "too much" but more than anyone
can ever receive. The generous givers.

Alix, inside your body of pears and peaches, and mine of a thick
leafy salad, is delicacy, yes. But never thinness.
Let us picket Weight Watchers.
And throw aside Fashion. Give us the rich chorus
of American drama. The substantial narrative, the loud Country-
Western singer, not the thin lyrics of an English past.
We took clotted cream and spread it over our bread. Butter,
meat, vegetables, too.
I will not starve myself
in order to dance on European yachts, for we have our
square dances here. And hoe downs. And most of all,
the dance of our daily bread.

Give us this day . . .
yes, and forgive us,
as we forgive those who want us to be thin. For this is the
kingdom.
Yes, and the power and glory
forever.

Ah, men.

(The sigh of a well-fed woman).

3 Feb 1976

Dear Debra

I am sure that you have probably been
        walking the San Andreas fault for cracks,
        writing poems in milk,
        finding lemons in the glove compartments of old Buicks,
        giving a few snakes a bath,
        letting the moon roll under the arch of yr foot,
        snipping roses off the ends of yr sleeve where they have
            been growing much too rapidly,
        and trying to keep from dropping yr violin,
and consequently, that is why you haven't written me a letter.

I understand how urgent these activities are, especially
along with
        keeping a close watch on the sky for meteors,
        and making sure Pat doesn't wrap too many water
            hyacinths around the towel racks in the bathroom,
        and assuring yrself that Chris is actually using his surf
            board instead of spreading butterfly wings on the
            waves as he, foolishly, likes to do
        And while it is not yr concern, to keep everything
            shipshape,
you are always
kind.
      And don't want to refuse anyone
the poet's gesture of
caring.

Still, you might write me a line,
for the snakes I have been bathing lately

147

are turning as pale as milk,
and I'm afraid that lemon and heat will only turn them to
squiggles.
Like arabic or
sanscrit.
And the San Andreas fault of
my silly life
will finally crack into a tangle of those waxy pink hyacinths,
until only a silver ship of my fingers is left,
trying to type,
              "Hello, hello. Where are you? Write me.
Just a line."

                              yrs,
                              diane

My Aunt Eva who Collected More Than 5,000 Pairs of Salt and Pepper Shakers Before Her Husband Told Her He Wouldn't Buy Any More Cabinets for Them

Big bosom,
marcelled grey hair.
Always powdered, always
corseted, the most formal
of my relatives.
I loved her,
for, poor as she was,
and as little an intellectual
        (she was a hotel maid until she married
          Uncle Elmer, who looked like George Washington
          and was a waiter-cook in a diner until they moved
          to California, and thereafter, a laborer for the county
          roads
          department)
she maintained
a kind of formality,
even the elegance of formality
in her life.
I have only found that elsewhere in art.

I remember that she always smelled good.
I remember that she had a big diamond ring, even though they
    were poor.
I remember that she cooked navy beans very well.
I remember that she subscribed to and read *The Farm Journal*
    even tho

they did not live on a farm.
I remember the neatness of her house.
She also painted china.
She reminded me of the chaos of my life.
Of my mind, which I was always rearranging.

One of her grandsons is a policeman.

Perhaps the word "love" should not be used on this page,
or any page.
The crotches of the bare winter trees outside my window have
    nest-shaped
cones of snow in them. I would like to see a red-tailed hawk
sitting in one, but see only the reddish-yellow marsh glinting
under the grey trees. No
movement.
The day still, covered with crusting white snow. And I thinking
of the King of Spain trying to hitch a ride to the mid-west,
his gold tooth glinting as he smiles at truckers and Cadillacs,
thinking of the beach on which I am not walking,
and the man whom I love, who is not loving me,
and the palm trees where an oriole is flying right now,
and my Aunt Eva who is 81 and who has just decided she may
start collecting salt and pepper shakers
again.

Describe the Sky on a Postcard

The sky is not like my desk, which makes me nervous. So filled
with letters I cannot answer, stacked with books that should be
read and then talked about, filled with possibilities of jobs and
money, and worst, at the bottom, all the requests for poems that
either I am not ready to write or haven't organized myself well
enough to type up and send out. No, the sky is empty, even
when it is filled with clouds, for no one has to answer a cloud.
What is a cloud anyway? Not even as substantial as a poem.
How is it we become what we have always made fun of or
despised? The clouds in the sky today are like black dahlias.
Their edges are smooth and sharp. They contain rain; remind me
of my black silk shawl.

Sestina to the Common Glass of Beer:
I Do Not Drink Beer

What calendar do you consult for an explosion of the sun?
And how does it affect our poor histories?
The event might be no different to our distant perspective
than a whole hillside of daffodils,
flashing
their own trumpet faces; or a cup of coffee, a glass of beer.

A familiar thing to common people: a beer,
when it is hot, and the sun
flashing
into your eyes. Makes you forget history's
only meaningful in retrospect. While flowers, like daffodils,
only have their meaning in the fleshy present. Perspective

cannot explain sexual feelings, though. Perspective-
ly, viewing a glass of beer,
we compare the color to daffodils
and perhaps a simple morning view of the sun.
The appetite is history's
fact. Common. Dull. Repetitious. Not flashing.

Suddenly, without explanation. The routine of bowels and lips.
   Flashing
past like a train, they come. No previews or perspective.
Sexual feelings are unexplained, as unexpected beauty. History's
no good at telling us about love either. Over beer
in a cafe, you might stay up till sun-
rise, but even that's routine for some, as every spring the returning
   daffodils,

waxy, yellow as caged canaries, spring daffodils
make me want to touch them. Is this the flashing
disappearing feeling of love and sex the sun
also brings to my body? With no object, no other body's perspective,
only the satisfaction of self wanting completion? I wdn't order beer,
I'd order a cognac or wine, instead. History's

full of exceptions, and I think I'm one. Yet, what history's
really about is how common, recurring, we all are. The daffodils,
once planted, really do come back each spring. And drinking beer
is a habit most ordinary men have. The flashing
gold liquid recurs in war, in factories and farms. The sun
has explosions that we do not know, record, or ever keep in
        perspective.

Thus, the sun embodies more of the unknown than most human
        histories.
We get little perspective outside ourselves. Daffodils
lift me above (to the sun), the faces flashing
each springtime when my friends, not I,
sit in some bar or outdoor cafe,
drinking beer.

George Washington's Camp Cups

>   "Be kind to yourself," she said
>   last February. "Don't forget
>   the small things. The good
>   book. The cup of tea."

And that winter at Valley Forge
was one
we must all weep to remember.
Shoes ragged,
coats growing thin.
The food diminishing. Meal full of rot
and worms.

General Washington, my father,
for his comfort,
had sixteen silver dollars cast into cups,
small cylinders for drinking
grog,
sailor's drink,
soldier's fuel.
And I suppose some would sneer, with revolutionary zeal,
at his looking to his own comfort
when men were starving,
freezing,
>   ("Eat yr vegetables, dear.
>   Think of the starving children in
>   India.")

The same ones who sneered at me in the '60s.

154

("How can you write poetry
when the world is falling apart?")

As if,
somehow,
this were the first time
the world had been
falling apart,
and there were something I could do
to mend that great tearing.

Surely not,
tho?
Or how could we be here, spinning
with silver bombers,
and heavy lead feet out walking on the moon's powdery surface?
In this age of technology,
I wonder that
Humpty Dumpty was so impossible to put back together
again,
for tho he would have been ragged and scarred,
and not the old innocent egg,
surely, there are means of rescuing,
recycling?

Change?
Growth?
Have we ruled them out of the world? Must
only the smooth,
the brand new
be viable?

"Be kind to yrself.
Don't forget the small things.
The good book.
The cup of tea."
But oh, the pain of that admonition,
reminding of the difference between an adventurous vacationer
exploring exotic Elba,

and that broken crumpled toy soldier who was exiled
there.

I have drunk thousands of cups of tea
this year.
And from George Washington's camp cup,
lots of grog.
The mid-West hears me reading books
while, like a siren, my voice floats over the waves at Laguna Beach.
No ideas of order,
but thoughts of love, of losing it,
                                        of the pain.
George's men were starving,
freezing,
in a fight most were too young to understand.
He, writing his letters every morning at 4 a.m.,
his warm grog steaming out of the silver dollar cup.

Outside a winter window,
the King of Spain,
not properly dressed for a blizzard,
in his gold shoes, thin silks and frozen mustache,
still leaves his footprints.

"Be kind to yrself," I admonish everyone,
waiting for my cup of tea.
And I wait for the King of Spain,
dreaming of George, my father,
of Beethoven who rescued me,
of David who is dead and buried on a California beach,
and of all the beautiful men I have loved;
for loving is
the secret; not
being loved.

What virtue in the egg's new smoothness,
except the beauty of perfection in birth;
I want to see Humpty Dumpty put back together again,
to love him for his ragged, jagged edges,

and the yoke scrambled with white.
Evidence of living.
Evidence of life.

George, I toast you.
M, I love you.
Beethoven, I want to hear you at Key West.
Be kind
to yrself,
all of you.
Don't forget the small things.
The good book.
The cup of tea.
An egg, put back together again, not
by magic,
but by patience, effort.
Love.

Printed October 1976 in Santa Barbara & Ann Arbor
for the Black Sparrow Press by Mackintosh & Young
and Edwards Brothers Inc. Design by Barbara Martin.
This edition is published in paper wrappers; there are
500 hardcover trade copies; 250 hardcover copies
numbered & signed by the author; & 50 numbered copies
handbound in boards by Earle Gray, each containing an
original holograph poem by Diane Wakoski.

Photo: Thomas Victor

Diane Wakoski was born in California in 1937. The poems in her published books give all the important information about her life.